P9-DMU-103

TABLE OF CONTENTS

THE HAT

Virginia Avery's "Easter bonnet," made by Shirley Botsford, is decorated with sewing notions.

This hat from Thailand is constructed with four-sections in green, gold, red, and fuchsia. Each section is decorated with a yarn rosette in the center that is held in place with half-dome silver beads. It is heavily quilted.

THE HAT

The hat! The hat! The marvelous hat! What fun you can have with a topper! Throughout fashion history, hats have been a major force, usually cooperating with or emphasizing a hair style as well as a garment. Hats, those priceless little additions, are indispensable grace notes of chic. They embellish our image and adorn our basic clothes. More than that, they are quick, simple, easy to sew, and we need look no further than our own fabric stashes to get started. Many of you could put together a stunning hat in less time than it takes to find a parking place at the shopping mall, and you'd have more fun doing it. I'll show you how to create hats plus give you examples to spark your own ideas.

For years, I've encouraged women to use their little leisure or discretionary time for the greatest benefit: sewing something special for themselves. Such garments transcend fad; they are classics. Hats fall into this category, for they can be worn with plain clothing to change the look and mood of the moment. Hats make your wardrobe work. They can be as simple or as detailed as you want. They are small enough to fit in a tote bag for a fast change later on. Packed for travel, they take up little space but offer maximum change—easier and cheaper than bringing or buying several different outfits! Their biggest attraction, however, is creating them. Almost any fabric is suitable, and fabrics can be combined extravagantly for texture and color effects. Hats offer you the perfect medium for embellishment: baubles, bangles and beads of all kinds, laces and ribbons, feathers and shells, exciting new threads for stitching. So dig into your stash and get started. Hats have the magic power to change any basic outfit from plain to fancy, and back again. They suit any mood, any occasion, any event. What more could we ask?

Hats fit all personalities and whims. There is no boundary to hat design. You'll see big-brimmed hats, big crowns, mushroom and lampshade-styled hats, the ubiquitous baseball cap, the pillbox, and some soft hats which look (deliberately) as though they've been sat or rained on. You'll need a sense of humor or adventure to wear some hats. Others can give you mystery and sophistication—a beguiling appeal impossible to resist. Remember, too, that men really love to see women in hats, so wear your hats with everything!

WHAT YOU'LL NEED

If you've been sewing or mending, making quilts, clothing, or gifts, you probably have all basic supplies at hand with some left over. For reference, they are:

1. Rotary cutter and mat
2. Ruler for rotary cutter
3. Good sharp shears for cutting fabric and good sharp smaller scissors for trimming
4. Tape measure
5. Pins and thimble
6. Marking pencils or chalk
7. Seam ripper
8. Tracing and pattern paper
9. Masking or cellophane tape
10. Assorted needles and threads—metallics, rayon, machine embroidery threads, variegated threads, perle cotton, regular sewing thread
11. Glue stick and Tacky Glue®
12. Wonder-Under®, heavy Pellon®, buckram, thin batting, cotton flannel, unbleached muslin
13. Assorted fabrics for hat construction
14. Millinery or 20 gauge wire for hat brims
15. Grosgrain ribbon for finishing inner headband
16. Sewing machine in good working order, hopefully capable of double needle and free-motion stitching; extra needles, extra bobbins, and a zipper, darning, and embroidery foot
17. Metal Celtic bar to construct Celtic bias tape
18. Cording or butcher twine to construct piping
19. Assorted embellishments (buttons, yarn, flowers)

These are fairly standard supplies for any sewing room. You certainly won't need all of them for a project, but sooner or later you'll use them. If you can't find millinery wire, stitch 20 gauge wire to the outer edge of hat brims to give them shape. An unfamiliar item may be the belting ribbon; it is used primarily in hats. It is very similar to grosgrain but has a sawtooth edge. However, grosgrain ribbon, which is readily available, will do nicely.

There are so many brands of sewing supplies in the market place that you have plenty of choices. Over the years I've developed several favorites, and so many students ask me what I use that I want to mention them here. My favorite sewing machine is the Bernina®. It performs for me and I can count on it. I've used Coats and Clark threads for years with

This hat is worn by Chinese women in villages outside the walled city of Kathing, near the Kowloon border. It has a flat, woven straw brim and is quite stiff. The inner edge is bound in black. A 6" strip of finely pleated black cotton, with a loose weave, is stitched around the outer edge. Twisted straw ties are under the chin to hold the hat in place.

⊗ FINDING YOUR HEAD SIZE

Finding your size is easy enough: Hold a tape measure rather snugly around your head, then add ½" to the measurement for ease.

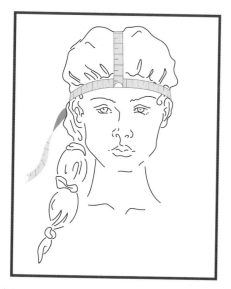

Determine the depth of the hat you need by using the above tape position as your guide, then measure over the top of your head.

great success. Their metallic thread was the first I could use in the needle assembly of my machine (instead of the bobbin) and it opened up a new world. Coats and Clark also has a good assortment of trims, braids, and other goodies. There are many good threads and notions available in the market today; whatever you use, keep your equipment and supplies in good working order. You can't turn out a good project without good equipment!

I did not list a pin block, for you probably won't be able to find one. It is a light, wooden head (usually made of balsa) that is relatively inexpensive. You use it to drape, mold, or fit hats over, then stick pins into—hence the name. These blocks used to be sold at all millinery supply houses, but are now hard to find. If you do find them, they come in head sizes, so you should know your size (see below).

There are a couple of adequate substitutes for a pin block. One is a wig stand, available in beauty supply houses or wig shops. These Styrofoam® heads are very light, and they will do nicely if you want to support your hat while you're working on it. The wig stands aren't sized, so you'll have to compensate to get the right fit. The other substitute is a plastic bowl from your kitchen. When you're not using it for cooking, turn it upside down and drape a hat on it! Try on a bowl or two, and pick the nearest to your size.

FINDING YOUR HEAD SIZE

Knowing your head size will help you adjust the hat patterns for a correct fit and achieve the desired look. Determine your head size by holding the tape measure snugly across the forehead, then around to the back of the head, positioning the tape to cover the top of the ears. Add ½" for ease. A small head size is 20" to 21", a medium 21" to 23", and 23" upward is large. Find the depth of the hat you need by using the first tape position as your guide, then measure over the top of your head.

THE FABRICS

There's hardly any fabric you can't use for hats! Almost anything you can get a needle through will do, and do nicely. Lightweight wools, challis, jersey, and crepes are soft and easy to work with, and they drape beautifully. If you use them for a structured hat, you'll have to support them with interfacing or fillers. Heavy silks hold their shapes well, and lighter silks can be draped, pleated, tucked, wrinkled, or quilted. Cottons, of course, are faithful and dependable. They are available in many weights and come in solids and a variety of prints and finishes. Ultrasuede®, Facile® (now known as Ultrasuede® Light), as well as felt, are good choices, but so is Ultraleather®, and the real thing, if you happen to have it. Velvet, brocade, and corduroy adapt well, and so does panne velvet, particularly since the pile is not directional. Mexican and Guatemalan cottons are hand woven, sturdy, and offer a bright palette. African cottons are bold and dramatic; batiks from Indonesia are stunning and inviting. Denims, velveteen, and decorator cottons are heavier fabrics and work well with hats. There are hand-dyed and painted fabrics available today; if you are so inclined, you can create your own. Finally, don't forget men's ties. Take them apart, wash them to get out the gravy and ketchup stains, press, and they're ready.

Most of my garments are made on a foundation fabric; unbleached muslin and cotton flannel (both pre-shrunk) are two stand-bys, but so is Fairfield Processing's Cotton Classic® batt. It is a thin batt, 80% cotton and 20% polyester, doesn't beard, and works wonderfully in clothing because it drapes beautifully. I've also split it to use in some garments, but fleece or other thin batting can also be used.

You can change the character of your fabric by pleating, wrinkling, slashing, stitching, or quilting it. The best news of all is that you can make almost any style of hat from a yard or less of fabric. (The yardage in the material lists is based on a 44" width unless otherwise noted.) You know, of course, your fabric talks to you, so listen carefully and you may hear it say, "Use me in a hat."

THE PATTERNS

Within this book, you'll find a pull-out sheet of hat patterns. A hat is relatively simple to make; consequently, the pattern section is simple, too. Where only half the pattern is shown, place the fold line of the pattern on the fold of the paper, then trace and cut. The hat patterns in this book are sized for a medium head, but you can easily adjust the measurements. Add or subtract by $\frac{1}{2}$" increments to adjust the pattern size. A word to the wise: Make a trial hat of muslin or scrap fabric and try on for size, then make any adjustments.

THE PATTERNS

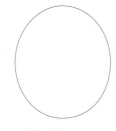

Top Crown

Crown Band

Six-Section Crown

Starfish Crown

Full-Circle Brim

The outside circle is the full-circle brim, mob cap, and large beret circumference. The center circle is for the small beret. The inner circle is the head opening.

The crown of the hat is the part that fits over your head. It can be one piece of fabric pleated or gathered into the seam which joins the crown to a brim. Or it can be made of two or more sections. The two-section crown has a top and a band (these are labeled top crown and crown band). This type of crown is a hat all by itself—think of the pillbox. The top crown can be round or oval. The pattern on the pull-out is for an oval crown. For a round top crown, draw a 9 1/4" diameter circle for the pattern. The crown band can be as narrow as 2" or as wide as 11"; it is very versatile. Cut it on either the straight or the bias grain, then depending on the desired effect, pleat, twist, or quilt it, or leave it alone. The crown band can also be strip-pieced, crazy-pieced, or appliquéd. The six-section crown is made of pie-shaped pieces seamed together, a "starfish" crown is made when you exaggerate the pie-shaped pieces.

There are several brim patterns in the pull-out section. The largest is the full-circle or cartwheel brim. It can be any width you want, as long as it is a flat circle. Usually this brim needs to be wired to hold its shape. The shaped brim is smaller, and to get a good idea of how it is formed and what it will do, first cut the brim pattern from the paper (cut out the head opening, too). Now fold a pleat on each side, the front, and the back; it's easy now to see how the shape changes. The more pleats or darts you take in the paper pattern, the more you change the shape.

There are several visor brim patterns as well. The peak (as in Rita Zerull's Sun Visor, page 21) goes all the way around the head, then is tied or sewn at the back. The familiar visor brim of baseball hats goes only around the front. Visor brims need to be stiff, so I use a couple of layers of buckram, fleece, or heavy interfacing in the construction.

There are patterns for an 11" and 15" beret, though you hardly need them. Berets consist of two circles. A solid circle is used for the top crown. The second circle (the crown band) is the same size, but it has a hole in the middle to accommodate the head. The hole varies by head size. The edge of the hole opening is finished with binding or a band.

The mob cap is similar in appearance to the beret, but the construction is different. The mob cap is two big circles placed together, wrong sides facing, with the edges bound. About 2 1/2" or 3" in from the edge, two parallel lines are stitched an inch or so apart to form a casing for the elastic. When the elastic is drawn up to fit the head, the mob cap becomes a blousy crown with a gathered brim.

Anita Murphy's turban pattern is for the type of turban permanently sewn in place, usually over a foundation cap or lining. Turbans are wrapped hats, usually made of squares, rectangles, or strips of fabric. Some are wound around the head, crossed in front, and the ends are tucked under the twists. An alternative is to tie the ends in an exaggerated knot at the front.

I haven't included a pattern for the tube, because it is so easy to make. The tube hat is just what it says—a tube. A tube hat, for maximum effect, is a wide tube, 11" or more. The extra width gives you the opportunity to drape it in interesting ways before trimming it. The excess can also be pulled to the top of the head and tied with ribbon or cord to hold in the gathers.

Many of these patterns can be combined or substituted for variety. For instance, a six-section crown can be worn alone, have a peak, visor, or cartwheel brim. Don't be afraid to experiment.

Shaped Brim

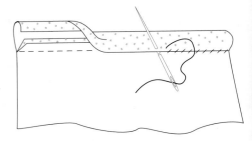

Peak or Sun Visor

Visor Brim

THE TECHNIQUES

Most of the techniques you use in hat making are simple: they are the same ones used in making a quilt or a garment.

FINISHING A SEAM

There are two main seams in making a three piece hat. The first seam joins the top crown to the crown band, the second seam joins the crown band to the brim. Finish any exposed seams by covering the raw edges with binding. An alternative to binding is to hold the edge of lining back, without catching it in the seam, then turn under this edge and hand-stitch it over the seam, covering it. Binding hat seams is just like binding quilt edges or garment seams; binding cut on the bias is easier to work with and will go around any shape. Bindings may be single or double, but I prefer the French double binding. The French double binding may be cut from almost any fabric, but always on the bias. The binding strip is four times the finished width *plus* two seam allowances. For instance, a finished ¹/₂" binding with a ¹/₂" seam allowance needs a strip 3" wide. After cutting it, fold the strip in half lengthwise, wrong sides facing, and press lightly. Match the raw edges of the bias strip to the raw edges of the seam to be covered, then sew through all thicknesses. Turn the folded edge over the seam then slipstitch the folded edge along the seamline.

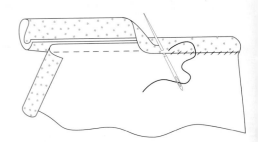

Attaching single binding

Attaching French double binding

WIRING A HAT BRIM

Another technique which may be new to you is wiring a hat brim. You won't do this often, probably only on wide or soft brims which need some reinforcement and shaping. Cut the wire (millinery or 20 gauge) a couple of inches longer than the outside circumference of the brim. Depending on the hat style, there are several methods to attach the wire.

One method is to seam the upper and lower brims together, right sides facing. Trim the seam if necessary, then turn and press. Slip the wire (with ends fastened together) inside the brim, pushing it as snugly against the seam as possible, and pin it in place to keep it from slipping. Now, with a zipper foot on your machine, topstitch through the brim, encasing the wire between the topstitching and the seam. This topstitching can be covered with braid or ribbon if you don't want it to show, or you can use a decorative stitch on the machine. An alternative method is to zigzag the wire to the outer edge, then cover the wire with binding, encasing it.

FINISHING THE INNER HEADBAND

Grosgrain ribbon is commonly used as the inner headband (the ribbon covers the seam which joins the crown band and brim). Grosgrain is easier to sew if you swirl or steam it into a circular shape first. Dip the ribbon in water, then pin it into shape on the ironing board and press. Let the ribbon dry for a few minutes before removing it from the ironing board. Pin the ribbon over the seam and topstitch in place.

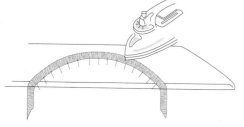

Swirl the grosgrain ribbon for the headband by first wetting it, then pin it into shape on the ironing board, and press until dry.

EMBELLISHING THE HAT

HATBANDS

Perhaps the most common embellishment is the hatband. This band covers the outer seam which joins the brim to the crown. It can be a simple bit of ribbon, a strip of fabric, braided cords, a twisted length of fabric, or a spray of feathers or flowers circling the hat. Anything goes. Added to the band, or in place of it, can be ribbon or fabric bows, fabric poufs, tassels, or fabric flowers. There are no rules.

FABRIC ROSES

Artificial flowers are readily available, but if you want to match or complement your hat with a certain fabric these roses are fast, easy, and fun to make.

Cut a strip of fabric; the length determines the size of the flower. Cut across the entire crosswise grain for a fairly large rose; use a 10"–12" strip for buds. The fabric may also be cut on the bias. Cut the strip twice as wide as the flower, since you'll be working with a folded strip. Fold the strip in half lengthwise, wrong sides facing and matching the edges. Run a basting thread from one end to the other, curving the stitches from the bottom edge up to the fold at each end. The folded edge of the strip may be left as it is, or zigzag over the edge with metallic thread for a bit of shine. Trim off the corner excess fabric. Pull the basting thread until the entire strip is gathered evenly. To start the rose, fold one end at a right angle to the bottom edge; a pencil will help in rolling. If you want stamens in the flower center, now is the time to add them. Start wrapping the flower, hand tacking it in place as you go. When you come to the end of the strip, tuck it under the rose so no raw edges show. Tack the flower securely at the bottom. To cover the raw edges, cut a small square or circle and sew over the rose bottom. Make as many flowers as you need for trim.

Another option is to create the roses with wired ribbon. These roses, in different sizes, make a wonderful bouquet to embellish the entire hatband. As a general rule, use 24" of 2 $\frac{1}{2}$"-wide ribbon to make a medium rose.

Fold the strip in half lengthwise, and gather along the raw edges. The dashed line is the basting thread. The zigzag stitch along the fold is optional.

Starting at one end, wrap the strip around a pencil, tacking the gathers in place as you go.

When the rose is wound, secure the bottom with extra stitches.

To cover the raw edges, sew a fabric square, or circle, over the rose bottom.

FLOWER PETALS

Use one or more of the leaf patterns in the pull-out section, or draw your own to make flower petals. Choose two fabrics, one each for the petal top and bottom. (Your flowers don't have to be all the same color or the same fabric!) Bond the fabrics together, wrong sides facing, with fusible web. This fusing also helps support the flowers. Place the patterns on the fabric in any direction (I don't pay attention to the grain) and cut the petals. Machine zigzag or straight stitch around the petal edges, then cluster them together to form the flower. Tack the flowers securely at the bottom. Sew a bead or button in the center.

When using the shapes for leaves, stitch in the veins.

Five-petaled flower with bead center

Layered petal flower

⊙ EMBELLISHING THE HAT

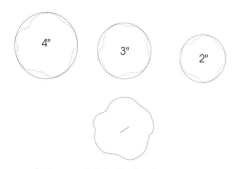

Cut a small slit in the bottom fabric.

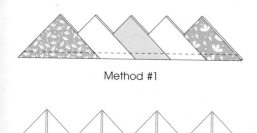

Stacked Flower

STACKED FLOWERS

The stacked flower is made from irregular circles—whoever heard of an irregular circle?—in three sizes: 4", 3" and 2". You may use other sizes if you prefer.

You'll need six different fabrics (two for each circle). Trace each circle on the wrong side of three fabrics. The wiggly line inside the circle is the sewing line; you don't need to draw it on the fabric. Put the fabrics with the drawn circles over another fabric, right sides facing. Using the circle as your guide, stitch the two fabrics together inside the circle, making your sewing line wiggly as shown in the illustration. Trim the seam closely, then make a little slit in the center of one side (this will be the bottom of the flower circle). Turn the flower through the slit and press. Repeat for each of the circles. Stack them (slit side down) with the largest circle on the bottom, then the middle, and the smallest on top. Tack through the flower center and add a button or bead to cover the tack stitches.

PRAIRIE POINTS

Prairie points give a decorative touch to seams. Prairie points are triangles. I don't know where they got their name, but they've been around for a long time. Prairie points can be stitched in the binding along the outside edge of a hat brim, with the points upward. Or, if you want a sawtooth edging for the brim, point them downward, pinning the raw edge in place and covering it with bias or braid. There are two "real" ways to make them, and a third I devised, which I call a "fake" prairie point. They can be any size and used individually or in a row. A square of fabric is the basis for all.

For method #1, fold the square on the diagonal. You now have a triangle. Fold again on the diagonal to make a smaller triangle. Where the first bias folds come together there will be an opening. Pin this triangle across the raw edge to keep it from unfolding. Make a second triangle in the same way, but keep the bias fold opening to your right. Slip the other side of the triangle inside the opening of the first triangle, so that the bottom edges overlap. Repeat as many times as you want, pinning or basting along the bottom edges.

For method #2, fold the fabric square in half horizontally. This makes a rectangle. Mark the midpoint of the folded edge, then bring both halves down at right angles to the bottom. This leaves a little folded opening in the middle of the triangle rather than at the side. When you

Method #1

Method #2

use more than one in a seam or at an edge, you do not overlap them; the bottom corner of one just meets the bottom corner of the next.

My fake method requires sewing, but it goes very fast. Place two fabric squares right sides together. Machine stitch $\frac{1}{4}$" around all edges. Cut the squares in half diagonally, then turn and press. This gives you a faced triangle instead of a folded one. For added variety, use two different fabrics or colors for the prairie points.

TWO-TONED PRAIRIE POINTS

Carole Liebzeit makes an interesting two-toned prairie point, which she used on the pillbox she made for this book. First, cut 1 $\frac{3}{4}$"-wide strips from two contrasting fabrics. Place the strips together, right sides facing, and stitch across one long edge using a $\frac{1}{4}$" seam allowance.

Mark and cut the strip every 3". Fold the top half to the back so $\frac{1}{8}$" of the darker fabric shows across the edge, and press. This folded section will look like piping. The lower edges will not be even after pressing, so you'll need to trim them. Fold the section into a prairie point with the contrasting edges in the center.

Usually, when we stitch prairie points into a seam, we place them edge to edge or overlap them a little (although single prairie points are often used as accents). Carole goes a step further: For her tall prairie points, fold the two lower points toward the back on the dotted line, then stitch along the bottom edge to hold them in place. These prairie points have added height, and they are sewn into a seam singly, not overlapping. You can easily stitch them as a separate trim or use them in a row of points, with a slight space between each one.

COUCHING

Embellish plain, wrinkled, or textured fabric with couching. Couching is a method of attaching a length of cord, yarn, braid, or crosslocked beads to the fabric with thread, either by hand or machine. Arrange the couching yarns on the fabric in a design of your choice, then pin the yarn in place. For machine work, attach with free-motion stitching, open zigzag, or other decorative stitches. If you want to hide the couching stitches, use transparent thread when stitching.

Two-Toned Prairie Points

Seam together to make a band.

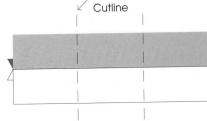

Straight cut into 3" sections.

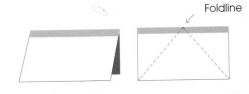

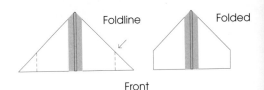

Front

A double layer of prairie points, with a ribbon covering the bottom edge

Free-motion couching stitch

Open-zigzag couching stitch

Herringbone couching stitch

EMBELLISHING THE HAT

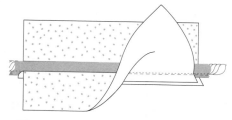

Stitch the piping into the seam. The piping may be any width. You can also stack your piping, sewing multiple layers into the same seam.

Wind the yarn around the cardboard.

Slip the yarn under the wraps and tie securely.

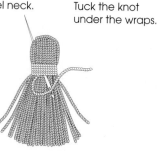

Wrap the tassel neck.

Tuck the knot under the wraps.

An alternative method is to tuck the needle under the neck and bring it through to the top.

PIPING

Piping adds an interesting touch to many seams. You can buy commercial piping, but often the fabric is not as good, or the color may be off. It's quite easy to make piping using your own choice of fabric. I use butcher twine (or rattail cord) for a thin piping and cotton cable cord (the kind of welting decorators use in slip covers) for thicker ones. Cut a strip of true bias wide enough to fit around the cord with enough added for seam allowances. Put a zipper foot on your machine and set it about 12 stitches to the inch. Fold the bias over the cord, pin the raw edges together, then stitch through the folded strip close to the cord, without catching it. Stretch the bias slightly as you sew.

TASSELS

Making your own tassels for embellishment is very easy. Start by winding a length of yarn or perle cotton around a piece of cardboard. The height of the cardboard determines the length of the tassel. The number of wraps determines the thickness of the tassel. When you have wound enough yarn around the cardboard, slide about 10" of yarn under one edge and tie securely. Remove the tassel from the cardboard and cut through the loops at the bottom; trim the ends evenly.

Wrap the tassel neck with matching or contrasting yarn or thread. Tie the ends of the yarn tightly and tuck the knot up under the wrapping. Alternatively, wrap over the beginning thread, then thread a large tapestry needle with the end of the yarn. Tuck the needle under the neck wraps and into the head of the tassel, bringing the needle up through the top. Add beads, charms or a few embroidery stitches over the neck for extra pizzazz.

Rita Zerull has passed on her method of making tassels from six strand embroidery floss, using a whole skein for each tassel. Here it is: Slip the paper rings off, leaving the floss intact. Fold the skein in half, then tie a 10" length of floss around the *midpoint* of the folded skein. This will be the tassel top. Fold the skein at the midpoint and wrap the neck. Add a bead or two if you like. Slip sharp scissors between the loops at the bottom and cut the strands. If the strands are uneven, give your tassel a trim. You now have a fat little tassel for embellishment. Use the ends of the 10" tie to fasten the tassel to the hat.

SOFT-SHAPED BRIM HATS

The soft-shaped brim hat has three parts: the top crown (oval or round), the crown band, and the shaped brim (patterns A, B, and C).

FORTUNE COOKIE HAT

The Fortune Cookie hat was the natural outcome of my frequent lunches with a friend at a neighborhood Chinese restaurant. When I'm not teaching somewhere, we meet, and we always order the same thing. We start with hot and sour soup, then share an order of moo-shu pork, drink lots of tea, and break open our fortune cookies. I had quite a collection of fortunes and wanted to use them somehow in clothing. Meanwhile, I was thinking about this book, and it seemed perfect to use the fortunes in a hat. I've used only good ones, so anything you read on this hat is highly complimentary. Because the hat is covered with plastic, it makes a whimsical rain hat complete with good reading material. You might use the same idea with theater or dance stubs, lottery tickets, bits of cards or letters, or any memorabilia which strikes your fancy.

1. Use patterns A, B, and C to cut the foundation from the black cotton. Arrange the fortunes on the top crown, crown band, and brim (as shown in the photograph) and hold them in place with a touch of glue. Next, cut clear plastic to cover. Machine stitch a grid through the plastic to hold the layers together, using a double needle with red and white threads. Cut the lining pieces from the polka dot cotton. All the pieces are now ready for assembly.

2. With right sides facing, seam the ends of the upper brim together, then press the seam open. Repeat this step for the brim lining. Place the brim lining against the upper brim, right sides facing, and stitch around the outer edge using 1/2" seam allowance. Trim the seams if necessary, turn, and press lightly. Topstitch 1/4" away from the outer edge to keep the brim from rolling. Set the brim aside.

3. With right sides facing, seam the ends of the crown band together and press the seam open. Sew the top crown to the crown band, using 1/2" seam allowance. Trim the seams if necessary. Repeat the construction steps for the lining pieces.

4. Slip the lining inside the crown unit, wrong sides facing, and pin or baste the lower edges together. Now pin the brim to the crown unit (upper brim facing right side of crown unit), matching the raw edges. Place a strip of bias binding against the brim lining, matching raw edges,

Fortune Cookie Hat

Materials for Fortune Cookie Hat
- Foundation fabric: 1/2 yard of black cotton
- Lining fabric: 1/2 yard of black and white polka dot cotton
- 1/2 yard of clear plastic
- Assorted paper fortunes or memorabilia
- Red and white sewing threads
- Glue stick
- Double needle (for machine)
- Embellishments: fabric roses (see page 11)
- Binding: 3/4 yard of 2 1/2"-wide bias

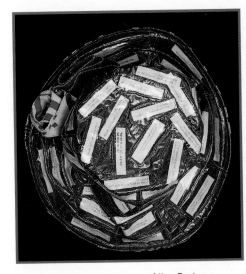

A look at the top crown of the Fortune Cookie Hat

SOFT-SHAPED BRIM HATS

1/4 " SEAM

With right sides facing and using a 1/4" seam allowance, stitch the ends of the upper brim together and press.

then stitch through all layers 1/2" from the edge. You will be stitching through seven layers here, so be careful; you don't want puckers or unplanned pleats caught in the seam. Trim the seams. Fold the bias up over the seam, turn under 1/2" seam allowance, and catch by hand to the crown band lining. The bias strip becomes the finished inner headband. For the final touch, add a couple of fabric roses.

Option: If sewing through seven layers is too much, you have an alternative. Pin the brim to the crown, but hold back the crown lining and do not catch it in the stitching. After sewing the brim to the crown, trim the seam and turn it upward inside the crown. Turn under the raw edge of the crown lining and catch by hand over the seam, covering it.

GUATEMALAN HAT

This hat is made from the same pattern pieces as the Fortune Cookie hat, only using Guatemalan fabric. The fabric is wonderful to work with. It's heavier than our "quilt" cotton, and it comes in striking colors. This hat is a collage of scraps stitched to a foundation.

1. Using the top crown pattern (A), cut one each from the black Guatemalan fabric, one from flannel (foundation), and one from the lining fabric. Using patterns B and C, cut one each from the foundation and lining fabrics. Lay the black Guatemalan top crown over the top crown foundation, matching the edges; baste together. Appliqué a 2" square of bright red and a 3 1/2 " piece of striped fabric to the black Guatemalan fabric.

2. For the crown band, arrange a collage of assorted pieces of Guatemalan fabric over the cotton flannel foundation. Zigzag the pieces in place with contrasting thread. Decorate the crown band using a free-motion zigzag stitch with metallic thread. The thread adds sparkle to the hat. If your machine does not have free-motion stitching, you can get the same effect by stitching back and forth with a straight stitch. Make the upper brim in the same manner.

3. Repeat step 2 of the Fortune Cookie hat, topstitching the brim 1/4" away from the outer edge with a machine feather stitch (to keep the brim from rolling). Repeat steps 3–4 of the Fortune Cookie hat, joining the brim to the crown with a seam piped in red. For the final touch, add a narrow Guatemalan hat band with little yarn puffs on the ends.

Guatemalan Hat

Materials for Guatemalan Hat
- Foundation fabric: 1/2 yard of cotton flannel
- Appliqué fabric: 1/2 yard total of assorted Guatemalan fabrics
- Lining fabric: 1/2 yard of black cotton
- Gold metallic thread
- 3/4 yard of red piping
- Guatemalan hatband (purchased)
- Binding: 3/4 yard of 2 1/2"-wide bias

FULL-CIRCLE BRIM (CARTWHEEL) HATS

This hat, and the Fortune Cookie hat, can be worn with the brim down all the way around, or turned up rakishly on one side or in front. You can make these hats in tweed, flannel, velvet, or corduroy for fall or winter. Use silks, cottons, brocades, or satins for other seasons or special occasions. You can strip-piece or quilt your fabric. Or, put one of Aunt Martha's crocheted doilies over the top crown. Catch the doily edges in place on the band with ribbon or fake pearls. These ideas will get you started and you'll have plenty of your own ideas—remember, it's all in having the right "Hattitude."

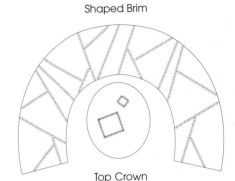

Shaped Brim

Top Crown

Crown Band

Raw-edge appliqué with free-motion zigzag. Lay the appliqué pieces on the foundation fabric with the raw edges butted together. Zigzag the edges in place, using contrasting threads.

FULL-CIRCLE BRIM HATS

These hats have long been associated with garden parties, "high tea," or romantic interludes. The brim is very feminine and suitable for weddings—worn even by the mother of the bride. It also makes a serious sun hat.

HIGH TEA HAT

None of us know when or where inspiration may strike. Until a couple of years ago, it certainly never occurred to me that I would ever need a high-tea hat, but then we held an American version of English high tea at our annual quilt camp. That first year, our hats were a hodgepodge, and no true Englishwoman would have ever been caught dead in any of them. The following year, we were all prepared. The hat in the photo is the one I made and wore while daintily consuming scones, clotted cream, jam, and tea. The fabric is a decorator cotton brocade in pale shades, and like the Fortune Cookie and Guatemalan hats it requires only three pieces. The top crown (A) and crown band (B) are the same as in the others, but the brim is the full circle, pattern D. The brim diameter is 15", but you can certainly have yours wider if you prefer. A narrow strip of lace forms the hatband and a nosegay of artificial violets against a lace doily is tacked to one side. You can use ribbon instead of the lace hatband, then decorate it with a corsage of fabric roses.

1. Using the top crown pattern (A), cut the lining, batting, and brocade. Make a sandwich of the pieces, the batt in the center. Free-motion quilt the top crown to within 1" of the outer edge. Set aside. Using the crown band pattern (B), cut out the band lining and batting. Cover the batting completely with scraps of fabric and try to get an interesting color composition. Cut two 6" x 60" strips of tulle. Now cover the band with a layer of tulle (you will have a 6" x 36" strip

High Tea Hat

Materials for High Tea Hat
- Fabric for brim and top crown: 3/4 yard of brocade
- Fabric for crown band: 1/8 yard total of assorted fabrics
- Foundation fabric: 1/2 yard of cotton batt
- Lining fabric: 1/4 yard of cotton
- 1/3 yard of 60"-wide tulle
- Binding: 3/4 yard of 3"-wide bias
- Embellishments: 3/4 yard of narrow lace, a nosegay, and a doily

FULL-CIRCLE BRIM (CARTWHEEL) HATS

remaining) and free-motion quilt through all layers. With right sides facing, seam the ends of the crown band together, using ¼" seam allowance, then press the seam open. Repeat for the band lining.

2. Place crown band and band lining together, wrong sides facing, then sew the crown band to the top crown, using ½" seam allowance and holding back the top crown lining. Turn the hat to the inside. Turn under the raw edge of the top crown lining, and hand stitch to the crown band, covering the seam.

3. Using the full-circle brim pattern (D), cut *two* of brocade and one of batting. Pin the batting to the wrong side of the upper brim. Then put the two brims together, right sides facing, and stitch around the outer edge using ½" seam allowance. Trim the seams, turn the brim to the right side and press.

4. Cut a length of wire slightly longer than the circumference of the brim. Overlap and twist the ends together securely. Slip the wire loop inside the brim up against the outside seam. Pin to hold the wire in place. With a zipper foot, stitch close to the wire to encase it. Then free-motion quilt the brim through all thicknesses to within 1" of the head opening.

5. Seam the short ends of the remaining strips together. Gather the inner edge to form a ruffle. Pin the ruffle to the upper brim. Staystitch ½" from the head opening. Trim the tulle close to the stitching and clip the inner brim edges at 1" intervals. Working from the underside of the brim, pin the brim to the bottom edge of the crown, matching the raw edges. Pin the folded bias binding around the opening. Stitch through all layers, ½" from the opening. Trim the seams, pull the bias up and over the raw edges, and hand stitch it to the inside of the band. Embellish the hat.

Pin the brim to the bottom edge of the crown, matching the raw edges.

MORE IDEAS

• As in the Mola Hat, you can substitute a triangle scarf instead of a crown. This triangle is of red cotton. I machine hemmed the raw edges and made it big enough so the ends would tie in back. The mola brim is lined with quilted cotton, the outer edge is wired, and both edges are bound. The long side of the triangle is stitched to the inside brim edge, leaving 4" free in back. The scarf ties cover this, and the scarf triangle is worn crushed to make a soft headband.

• Another idea for the crown is to gather a large circle of fabric around the outer edge, then pull the gathers up to meet the head opening. Pin in place, then sew the brim and crown together.

• For a dramatic dinner hat, cut the circle brim out of buckram, then wire the outside edge. Cut a strip of black chiffon twice the width of the brim plus two seam allowances. Sew the ends together so the chiffon forms a tube. Fold it in half lengthwise and slip the buckram brim inside. Gather up the raw edges of the chiffon to fit around the buckram brim, and hand tack it in place. Cut a circle of chiffon for the crown. Use a 12" circle so the crown will be very soft and unstructured. Gather the outer edge, and try it on. You want the crown to be fairly shallow, so it will help support the brim. Sew the brim and crown together and cover the seam with a black velvet ribbon. Add a bow, flower, or a pouf of veiling held in place with a rhinestone pin. You'll be a sensation.

• For a great summer hat, make a big wide brim, bind all the edges and trim with a garland of flowers around the head opening. This does away with the top crown entirely.

• Another idea is to weave an open crown with ribbon or fabric tubes, tack them together where they cross, then catch the ends in the seam between the brim layers.

The Mola Hat's brim is wired on the outer edge and is lined with orange quilted cotton. The mola design was planned to fit the circle shape. The triangular crown was stitched to the brim with the widest section in the front, and the ends tied in back. It is worn with the triangle crushed or draped around the head.

VISOR BRIM HATS

The baseball hat, along with T-shirts and jeans, is an established part of American fashion culture. But you don't have to play baseball or go to a game in order to wear one. They're used as an advertising medium and often given away with purchases. Painters and carpenters wear stiffened white ones, often with the name of a paint company emblazoned on them. Kids wear baseball hats. So do babies. Theirs are made of piqué or soft cotton and sometimes trimmed with ducks or bears. And, of course, teenage guys learning how to be macho wear them backwards. That's neat! That's cool! They're worn low over the forehead, and sometimes the brim is over one ear instead of the back. Grown-up women wear them too, of velvet or satin, cotton or wool, even sequins, although the hat is still sporty.

Three visor brim or baseball caps; the top hat is made of sequins, the lower left is from India and has hand-stitched gold braid, the lower right cap is made of African cotton.

VISOR BRIM HATS

Poppy Cap

Materials for Poppy Cap or Starfish Cap
- 1/2 yard of black, white, and red cotton print
- Interfacing: 1/4 yard of flannel
- Lining fabric: 1/2 yard of cotton
- 1/4 yard of heavy Pellon® for brim
- 3/4 yard of 5/8"-wide grosgrain ribbon
- Embellishments: fabric poppies for Poppy Cap

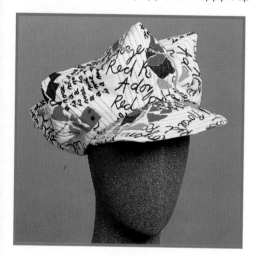

Starfish Cap

The dotted line shows the pattern for the six-section crown. The solid line shows the pattern for the Starfish Cap—note how the original shape was exaggerated.

POPPY CAP · STARFISH CAP

The two cotton hats pictured are made of the same fabric, a white cotton printed in black and red. I trimmed this baseball cap with a spray of poppies across the front, so I call it the Poppy Cap. This cap has a plain six-section crown. The Starfish Cap has a "starfish" crown—an exaggeration of the pie-shaped pattern piece. I named the crown starfish because after I finished it, it rather resembled a starfish—with six points instead of five. With either of these caps, if you're unsure of the size, pin the crown together first and try it on, then adjust if necessary.

1. For the Poppy Cap, you'll need crown pattern E and visor brim pattern G. There is no foundation fabric, just the outer fabric and the lining. Cut six crown pieces each from the fabrics. Using 1/4" seam allowance, stitch three crown sections together, then the other three, and join the two sections. It takes a little doing to keep the top flat where all the points converge. It's like sewing a star pattern in quilting—you don't want to end up with a hole in the middle or the points cut off. (If, in spite of everything, this happens anyway, sew a button or a tassel to the center top and don't worry about it.)

2. Repeat these steps for the lining, then slip the lining inside the crown unit, wrong sides facing, and pin the lower edges together. Stay-stitch 1/4" from the edge, through both layers.

3. Using pattern G, cut both the brim top and bottom from the cotton print and one from the cotton flannel. Baste the flannel piece to the wrong side of the upper brim. Stitch the upper and lower brim pieces together along the *outer* curve, right sides facing and using 1/2" seam allowance. Trim seams, turn and press.

4. Cut a layer of heavy Pellon®, trim the seam allowances, then slip it between the flannel and the brim lining. Quilt through all the layers. When attaching the visor brim to the crown, point the visor upwards over the crown, then pin right sides together and stitch, using 1/2" seam allowance. Finish with grosgrain ribbon, topstitching around the inner edge, covering the raw edges and the seam.

The Starfish Cap is slightly more complicated. Each of the outer crown sections is quilted to a layer of cotton flannel, then the sections are joined together. After stitching the lining together, slip it inside the crown and pin the bottom edges together, then stitch close to the edge through both layers. Make the brim the same as for the Poppy Cap. Topstitch grosgrain ribbon around the inner edge.

RITA ZERULL'S SUN VISOR

Rita Zerull passed on her recipe for a sun visor. She made hers of pieced Guatemalan fabric, appliquéd with a sun. Use pattern H for Rita Zerull's Sun Visor. Cut and seam the upper and lower brim pieces together around the outer edge, with right sides facing, then turn and press. Cut two layers of buckram (seams trimmed) and stitch the buckram layers together, then slip them inside the visor brim. Bind the inner edge; the binding extends to form the ties, which fasten at the nape of the neck. This visor, or peak brim, could also be used with a crown. Mix and match is the name of the game.

Rita Zerull's Sun Visor

Materials for Sun Visor
- Outer fabric: $5/8$ yard of pieced Guatemalan fabrics
- $1/2$ yard of buckram
- Binding: $1 \, 1/3$ yards of $2 \, 1/4$"-wide bias

BERETS

Beret the beautiful! It's a long-time classic, whether you like the big ones à la Scottish Highlands, the small ones à la Basque, or something in between. Berets are much loved hats, worn by both men and women. Big floppy ones are reminiscent of Scottish tam-o'-shanters. A small Basque beret is even more popular (with both sexes). When I see a person wearing one, I always think of a dashing Frenchman, beret on the side of his head, striding down the street in a belted trench coat with the collar turned up. Berets are romantic and mysterious but also useful and easy to make.

General Instructions for a Beret

1. A beret is made of two circles, one is the top crown and the other the crown band. The circle for the big beret is pattern D. (Yes, it's the same circle for the cartwheel hat brim.) The inner circle of the crown band is for a medium head measurement plus $1/2$" for ease. Adjust the head opening on the pattern D if needed. Cut the circle for the head opening from the crown band.

2. Stitch the two circles together on the outer edge, right sides facing. Repeat for the lining pieces. Slip the lining inside the beret, wrong sides facing and pin the edges together around the head opening. Since the head opening is a circle, the binding will be easier to attach if you staystitch $1/2$" from the edge, then clip the edge at 1" intervals. Bind the head opening of the crown band with bias (page 9) or braid. Or, if you prefer, cut a strip 3"-wide by the circumference of the head opening plus seam allowances. Interface this band to give it some body. Seam the ends together to make a ring, then fold it in half lengthwise and press. Press one raw edge to the inside $1/2$". With right sides facing and matching the raw edges, stitch the ring to the head opening. Fold the pressed edge over the seam and slipstitch in place.

The Big Beret is made of floral printed velveteen, and is piped in gold.

Materials for Big Beret
- Outer fabric: $1/2$ yard each of fashion fabric
- Foundation: $1/2$ yard of cotton batt
- Headband: 26" of a 3"-wide strip of interfaced fabric
- Lining: $1/2$ yard of black silk
- $2 \, 1/2$ yards of gold piping
- Gold metallic thread

BERETS

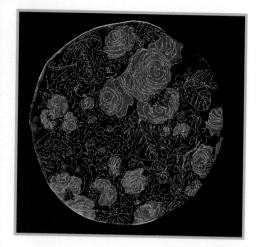

A detailed look at the Big Beret's crown. Note the free-motion quilting using gold metallic thread.

Small Beret

Materials for Small Beret
• Outer fabric: ¹⁄₃ yard of black and ¹⁄₄ yard total of four assorted corduroy fabrics
• Lining: ¹⁄₃ yard of cotton
• Foundation: ¹⁄₃ yard of cotton flannel
• Aluminum bars for Celtic bias strips
• ¹⁄₂ yard of print for bias strips and binding

Celtic Bias

BIG BERET

The big 15" beret in the photo is made of velveteen with roses printed on a brown background. Follow the general instructions above, but free-motion quilt the velveteen to the batting, using gold metallic thread around the roses. Insert gold piping into both seams of the crown band (see front cover photo); I used J.&P. Coats gold braid piping.

SMALL BERET WITH CELTIC BIAS

The small 11" beret is of very fine wale corduroy. Use the 11" cutting line on pattern D. Follow the general instructions, but pin the top crown and crown band together, wrong sides facing. Stitch the binding to the outside, covering the raw edges. The crown band is black corduroy, and the same cotton print is used in a regular bias binding on the outside of both seams. I've used what I call my "fabricage" technique in the design, with four different colors of corduroy with black as the main fabric.

Fabricage is a form of appliqué, but you don't have to turn under the raw edges. The shapes are simply butted together, or overlapped slightly (¹⁄₈" maximum) and stitched in place. The raw edges are covered with Celtic bias strips and topstitched in place on both sides near the edge. The bias adds to the design, and since it is bias and has that wonderful stretch, it fits around any curves or shapes.

Celtic bias is made using aluminum bars—not nylon or other substitutes. Philmena Durban developed this technique several years ago for quilts with Celtic designs—those intricate and detailed designs where you can't find a beginning or an end. I don't do Celtic designs, but I did adapt the bars for my own work, and they are indispensable. I use them for both stitching and pressing the tubes, which eliminates measuring and marking. The bars come in different sizes, so select the size you need.

Cut a true bias strip wide enough to fit around the bar, with an extra ¹⁄₂" on either side. Keep the raw edges of the fabric even, and pin every now and then the length of the bar—they are about 12" long. Put a zipper foot on your machine and stitch alongside the bar, through the fabric, stretching the bias slightly. If the bar isn't as long as your fabric, stop when you near the end, then leave the needle in the fabric strip. Simply slide the bar down and pin again to continue stitching.

When you've completed the stitching, trim the seam very close to the stitching line, then twist the seam from the side to the middle of the bias bar. Leave the bar in while you press. You now have a perfect bias strip ready to apply, and the seam will be concealed against the fabric when it's stitched. It's an easy, wonderful way to create a design.

• I listed some design ideas for you with the pillbox, but there are just as many or more with the beret. As you know, a flat surface offers you lots of opportunity for design. You can also divide the beret circle into sections if you like. For instance, if you want to divide it into four segments, simply fold a paper circle into fourths and trace around it. Then add the seam allowances. These segments could be alternating colors of four different fabrics, or you could strip piece them or use a quilt block design—as Shirley Botsford did.

Shirley Botsford made a soft, floppy, oversized beret using men's silk ties, with a wonderful pieced star pattern. Her star has eight points, but there are 16 sections in the crown. It is an unstructured beret, with elastic in the back to hold it snug on your head.

Here are a few more ideas to try:
• Stud your beret with fake jewels from the craft shop.
• Cover it with buttons, or couch it with twisted Christmas tree tinsel for the holidays.
• Use one fabric for the top, another for the crown band, and a third for finishing.
You get the idea.

Shirley Botsford made this big, floppy beret of tie silks. There is an 8-pointed star design at the crown center.

THE MOB CAP

It takes a certain type of woman to wear this hat, simply because we tend to associate it with English maids and Colonial dames. You need to have a lot of self-confidence. On the other hand, when this cap is made of velvets instead of white cotton, it really won't look like a maid's cap. It's just two big circles of fabric—no interfacing—stitched together and bound around the outside edge. Since the underside of the brim will be visible, both circles should be either the same fabric or two contrasting fashion fabrics, not lining material. This mob cap is full and blousy, so don't skimp on the size.

1. Cut the two big circles using pattern D. On one of them, mark a circle about 2–2 1/2" in from the outer edge (this becomes the brim width). Draw a second circle 1" or so inside the first. When stitched, the

The Mob Cap

Materials for The Mob Cap
• Outer fabric: 1/2 yard of fashion fabric
• 3/4 yard of 5/8"-wide elastic
• Binding: 1 5/8 yards of 3"-wide bias

PILLBOXES

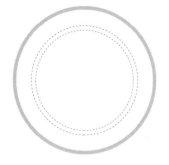

Stitch the parallel circles for the casing.

space between the two marked circles will depend on the width of your elastic. I think ⅝" elastic is wide enough.

2. Pin the two fabric pieces together, wrong sides facing. Sew the binding to the outer edge using a single or French double binding (page 9), covering the raw edges.

3. After binding, stitch the parallel circles for the casing. From the inside, make a little slit in the casing to thread the elastic through. Try the cap on and pull the elastic until you have a snug fit. Sew the ends of the elastic together securely and push it back inside the casing.

As I mentioned before, these hats are almost indestructible. You can squash them and abuse them, yet they always seem to spring back.

PILLBOXES

The pillbox has a long history. It's a perky little hat, and I'm not sure where it originated. It has shown up in most cultures, including ours, and I think it will stick around for awhile. Jackie Onassis gave it a boost, but it would have survived even without her nudging. Not long ago, I saw pictures of men wearing what looked like pillboxes—men from the Mountain Provinces. The hats, I found out, were more than pillboxes. They had pockets to hold the wearer's tobacco and matches. I read further that these men, of the Bontac tribe, live in a hot climate, and their entire costume typically consists of a girdle, a breech cloth, and a pocket hat. Gives you something to think about, doesn't it? Little pillbox hats are common in many parts of Africa. India has its own version. Romanian needleworkers make their pillbox hats from tapestry, needle-point, or heavy embroidery. We make them out of everything.

The first pillbox (1), created by Carole Liebzeit, is made from hand-dyed fabric. The crown is quilted for added support, and embellished with two-toned prairie points (page 13).

The next pillbox (2) is made of heavy decorator fabric, printed with a floral design. The lower edge of the crown band is defined with a 2" black strip of fabric which is seamed to the band.

The crown of this little Romanian needlepoint hat (3) is slightly different. Instead of being flat and round, it has a small dart which starts

These pillboxes (except Carole's) are from Judy Avery's pillbox collection; she bought some of them, but others she made.
Top row from left:1, 2, 3, 4
Bottom row from left: 5, 6, 7, 8, 9

Materials for Pillboxes
•Outer fabric: ¹/₄ yard
•Lining fabric: ¹/₄ yard
•¹/₄ yard of stiffening or interfacing

from the back of the crown and ends almost at the middle; it gives a slight arch to the crown. The band is narrower, too, just 2", and lined with black cotton.

The next hat (4) is from India. It's made of yellow mirror cloth with shisha mirrors—bits of mica fastened to the fabric with colored embroidery and highlighted with white seed beads. There is a blue embroidery stitch around the crown, band, and lower edge.

You'll notice that some of the bands are much wider than the others. The African hat (5), of gold cotton, has a 6" band. It's decorated with bands of red rickrack and black braid. The gold cotton is quilted, as is the outer band. The seams are finished with a zigzag edge. This hat sits high on the head, with a tuck in the band if worn lower.

The next hat (6) is a little hat from Nigeria, called a "fela". It is made of blue-green and silver glitz fabric and stitched heavily with close black circles. The band is only about 3 ¹/₂" wide.

The pillbox from Afghanistan (7) is made of hand-embroidered fine gold wire, sewn together in intricate patterns. The handwork is really amazing.

The black silk pillbox (8) has a wide gold braid appliquéd in a triangular design and set off with gold rickrack.

This last pillbox (9) is of printed wool challis in red, orange, and black. It's embellished with amber glass beads, small gray metal beads, and clusters of red beads. The lower edge of the pillbox turns up about

PILLBOXES

½" and is finished with gold cord next to the seam. A length of red velvet ribbon goes around the hat and finishes in a bow.

These small pillboxes wouldn't take long to make, and could be decorated any way you like. These hats (except Carole's) are from Judy Avery's pillbox collection; she made some of them, but others she bought.

General Instructions for the Pillbox

1. Use patterns A and B for any pillbox you wish to make. Pattern B is for a 4 ½"-wide crown band. Remember the crown band may vary from 2" to 11" wide. Depending on the fabric, you may have to add stiffening to the band so it will hold its shape. Using the pattern pieces, cut one each from the outer and lining fabrics.

2. Seam the short ends of the crown band together, right sides facing and using ¼" seam allowance; press. Seam the short ends of the crown band lining together, right sides facing and using ¼" seam allowance. Sew the lower edge of the crown band and band lining together, right sides facing and using ½" seam allowance. Trim the seams, turn and press. Baste the upper edges together. Sew the top crown to the crown band, right sides facing, and stitch using ½" seam allowance. Turn the lining of the top crown under ½" and hand stitch to the crown band, covering the seam.

MORE IDEAS

• The Corsage Pillbox doesn't really look like a pillbox because the band has a big tuck in the side with the corsage. It's a wide band, and the fabric itself is elegant. It's textured or pleated in antique golds, purple-red, and black. It looks rather like a watercolor painting, with all the colors running together. This is a soft hat, with no filler or interfacing, that fits snugly on the head.

You probably have a lot of ideas from the hats shown on page 25, but here are a few others you might want to try:
• Layer faced fabric circles for the top crown. Start with a 6" or larger circle and decrease the circles by 1" each time. Anchor the layers in the center with a button, bead, or tassel.
• Use one of your leftover quilt blocks for the top. Lay the top crown pattern over the block, cut around it, then use the scraps to appliqué on the band.
• Stitch circles of narrow fringe (1" wide) all over the top crown,

Corsage Pillbox

starting in the center. Do the same for the crown band.

• Crinkle your fabric, then stitch the crinkles in place over a base fabric, or iron the crinkled fabric to fusible interfacing. Couch (page 13) rattail or other cords or yarns over the surface.

• Quilt the fabric for your hat using hand or machine free-motion stitching, or machine stitch in close rows, using the presser foot as a guide.

• Decoratively apply rickrack and other braids.

• Weave fabric tubes into a pattern and use them for the top and band; the edges of the tubes will be caught in the seams and secured. You can do an open-work pattern over a contrasting base fabric, or a closely woven design which would not need a base.

• Cover the pillbox with tiny tassels made from six-strand embroidery floss (see page 14).

TURBANS

SCARF TURBAN

In many cultures, hats still have a ritual significance. They serve to identify and communicate, and they are very effective in this role. The Tzut, worn by the men in Chichicastenango, Guatemala, is an example. It is a head covering (not a true hat), but it bears a slight resemblance to some of our turbans. The Tzut is a large hand-woven square, decorated in symbolic patterns representing mountains, waters, sky, land, morning, and evening. Each design has a meaning. The corners of the square are tasseled. When worn, it is folded as a triangle and tied in back.

We do this too, but if the square is big enough after tying, we twist the ends and wind them back around our heads and tie them in front. We do much the same with long scarves but, because of the length and shape, they make better draped turbans. The only drawback is that each time you wear one of these you have to drape it all over again. Such scarves are about 14" wide—wide enough to fit over your head. If you put a few gathers or pleats in the front where the scarf meets your forehead, the turban will fit better.

Cross the scarf ends in back, then twist and wind around your head to the front. Cross the ends again, knot them, then tuck the tails into the twists.

Stitch gathers or pleats across the top front edge to make the turban fit better

Cross the ends again, knot them, then tuck the tails into the twists.

27

TURBANS

Turbans by Anita Murphy

Materials

• Outer fabric: ⅓ yard of soft jersey, double knit, fleece, or velour that has built-in stretch, so you won't have to pay any attention to grain. Use ⅝ yard of cotton or other woven fabric, and place the pattern pieces on the bias grain.
• Lining fabric: same as above

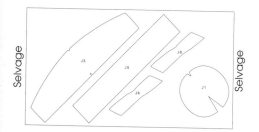

Layout for woven outer fabric of Anita Murphy's soft-draped turban

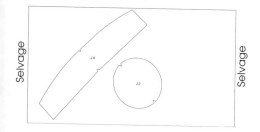

Layout for lining fabric

ANITA MURPHY'S SOFT-DRAPED TURBAN

Anita Murphy is a charming quiltmaker and sewer from Texas. She has come up with a soft and practical turban. It is wonderful to jam down onto your head when your hair is messed up or when it's snowing outside. She used to wear them to cover rollers (remember them?) in her hair. Another practical and poignant use is to wear one when chemotherapy treatments have done their worst. Anita made the trio of turbans in the photo, and she generously gave me the pattern to pass on to you. She said she made 24 of them in one day, so you have to believe they are fast and easy! Anita used gray double knit for one and trimmed it with a heart-shaped ornament. She recycled some jeans for the denim one and added a fringed denim flower. For the third, she used leftover fabrics from previous projects.

The patterns for the turban are in the pull-out section. Notice that the top crown (J1) has a dart in the back. It is also notched for matching in front. The crown lining is slightly smaller and has no dart (J2). The crown band (J3) outside is wider than the lining (J4), but has a tuck which makes the band look as if it is cut in two pieces.

The headband pattern, J5, is a length of fabric folded lengthwise and attached to the turban crown. Finally, there is pattern piece J6, a tie, which is a shaped and faced fabric piece. This tie, or knot, is attached at the back. When stitching across the middle of the tie, take a little tuck in the turban itself for a snug fit. After attaching the tie, pull the tie ends into a knot.

1. For the turban lining, cut one each of J2 and J4. Seam the ends of J4 together. Match the front notch at the top of the band to the front notch in the crown; pin and sew the pieces together.

2. Cut one each of J1, J3, J5, and two of J6 from the outer fabric. Stitch a dart in the back of the top crown with a ½" seam (tapering to the end point). Fold the crown band in half lengthwise, right sides facing, and stitch a ¼" tuck the length of the band. This tuck is purely decorative, you can insert prairie points or piping, etc. Unfold the band, then seam the ends with ½" seam allowance and press the seams open. Match the notch at the top of the crown band with the notch in the top crown, then stitch the band to the crown, easing fabric where necessary. Remember, the curved side of the band is the top and the straight edge is the bottom. The seam of the crown band should match the back dart in the top crown.

3. Place the lining inside the turban, wrong sides facing and matching the lower edges, then pin together. Set aside. Seam the ends of the headband together, using ¹/₂" seam allowance. Press the seam open then fold the band in half lengthwise, wrong sides facing and matching raw edges.

4. Starting at the back, pin the headband to the turban with the band next to the lining; after stitching the seam, conceal it by draping the crown band over the seam.

5. With right sides facing and using ¹/₄" seam allowance, sew the ties (J6) together, leaving an opening for turning. Turn, stitch the opening closed, and press. Sew the tie center to the center back seam. After attaching the tie, work the ends into a knot.

• You can make a really elegant draped turban using a pin block or wig stand. Draping is fun. There aren't any set rules, but if you use bias strips about 5" wide, they can be twisted and turned in any direction on the base frame, then tacked in place.

THE TUBE

MANHATTAN SUNSET

The tube hat is a little like a stocking cap, except that the fabric is far more elegant—and it isn't knitted. Manhattan Sunset, the silk tube hat in the photo, was made to complete my outfit for Fairfield Fashion Show in 1992. It's made of red and purple Thai silks and quilted with gold metallic thread. The hat is just a tube, 11" x 23", of red silk quilted to a thin batt, then lined with purple silk.

1. Cut an 11" x 23" piece each of cotton batting and red and purple silk. Quilt the red silk and batting together, then seam the ends together to form a tube. Seam the lining ends together to form a tube. Put the two tubes together, right sides facing, and stitch both sides, leaving an opening on one side. Turn, press, and hand-stitch the opening.

2. Now, decide how you're going to finish your hat. You can gather the crown tightly into a small circle, which would be the tip of the crown. Or tie with an ornamental cord and finish with a tassel. Another option is to pleat or gather the top of the tube, or do what I did—pull the tube down on one side and embellish it with flowers. The purple lining is visible from the side, too; it covers the seam but also adds to the design.

Manhattan Sunset

Materials for Manhattan Sunset
•Outer fabric: ¹/₂ yard of red silk
•Lining fabric: ¹/₂ yard of purple silk
•¹/₂ yard of batting
•Gold metallic thread
•Embellishments: fabric flowers and leaves (pages 11-12)

Although the hat is intended to be worn without a brim, you certainly could add one, and that would be very elegant indeed.

HEADBANDS

MARINDA STEWART'S HEADBANDS

If you think you don't have time to make a whole hat, or want a reasonable facsimile of one, buy some headbands and embellish them. The two in the photos were made by Marinda Stewart, a very clever West Coast designer.

The black and white Chanel Headband started with a purchased, padded headband 1 ½" wide. Marinda gathered together an assortment of black and white ribbons with some pearls as embellishments. The big bow has eight loops, and it is made of 1 ⅜"-wide organdy ribbon with black satin trim. The loops on either side of the bow are made of ¼"-wide black satin ribbon and ⅛"-wide black and white polka dot ribbon. All of these are attached to the headband with a glue gun. If you don't have one, try Tacky Glue®, white glue, or sew them in place with thread. Marinda made the gardenia trim from 1 ½"-wide white, satin wire ribbon with gold trim and glued it to the center of the bow. The flower center has one large pearl surrounded by seven smaller pearls, all glued in place. She added a ribbon rose and some leaves, and the result is fit for any evening out.

The Button Headband is based on a 1"-wide purchased, padded headband and trimmed with an assortment of colored buttons. Marinda added a few pre-made satin rosebuds, and you could also add charms if you like. This is a sportier headband, one you might wear throughout the day, although there is no rule to keep you from wearing it in the evening. Marinda started at the top of the headband with larger buttons—some overlapped, some layered—until the entire headband was encrusted with buttons. Buttons have been a popular form of embellishment for a couple of years, and I'm sure you must have your own special button jar. Packages of odd buttons are often sold in notion stores if you need more, or ask your family and friends to help you out.

Chanel Headband

Button Headband

COVERING HAT FRAMES

I've given you plenty of ideas to get started on your own hat wardrobe, but I'd like to add one more idea. Millinery and some craft stores carry buckram hat frames. These are a whole piece, made of starched buckram molded to hold a certain shape. They are made to be covered with your choice of fabric. They are made for handwork, not machine, though you might be able to bind the outside edges by machine. Starting with the crown, take a piece of fabric large enough to cover the whole crown; fit it snugly over the buckram form and pin the pleats or gathers around the lower edge of the crown. Hand tack this in place, smoothing out the excess, then trim. Next, cover the brim. If it's fairly flat you can use two pieces of fabric, one for the top and for the bottom of the brim.

If you've used a straight length of fabric for this, you'll have excess to pin at the crown line. The raw edges, from crown and brim, can be covered with ribbon or a fabric tube, or you might add a garland of flowers completely around the hat. Bind the outer edge of the buckram brim.

A purchased buckram form to cover with your choice of fabrics.

IN CLOSING...

As you've discovered, accessories don't take much fabric. Chances are, you'll have all the supplies you need at hand. However, if you've ever yearned for an expensive cut of fabric and felt you couldn't afford it for a vest or jacket, you can splurge on a half yard and create a wonderful hat without a guilty conscience!

Also, I hope you've learned never to throw *anything* away. I hang on to all kinds of things. Some are good, some bad—but then, you never know when they will come in handy.

I also keep bracelets I no longer wear, single or broken earrings, old buckles from belts, odd closures from jackets, worn suede and kid gloves, some plastic charms from key rings, and all kinds of other things. I keep ribbons from gifts, and laces, and bits of old linens. Often I can't find them when I need them, but at least I know they're here *somewhere*.

There are, as you know, countless ways to cover your head, and in this little book we are barely scratching the surface. Perhaps, though, you can view your own fabric stash or go into a fabric store with a new glint in your eye. It's all in having the right Hattitude!

ABOUT THE AUTHOR

A self-taught quilt and clothing designer, Virginia Avery has been professionally active in the quilt world for the past 30 years. She has been featured as teacher, lecturer, and judge at major quilt conferences, guilds, universities, and art museums throughout the world. Virginia brings warmth and wit to her work, and shares enthusiasm and information without reservation. Her perception of individual creative needs ensures enthusiastic response from her students. Her award-winning work is represented in many public and private collections; among her one-woman shows are the Smithsonian Institution and the Textile Museum of Washington, D.C. For rest and relaxation, Virginia plays piano for eight men in a Dixieland Jazz band, the King Street Stompers. She feels strongly that jazz, quilting, and clothing design are sisters under the skin, for they are always improving on a theme.

Virginia Avery is also the author of *Nifty Neckwear*— a companion book that gives readers enlightening lessons in creating over a dozen fabulous collars of any size, fabric, and style—and *The Big Book of Appliqué, Quilts to Wear,* and *Wonderful Wearables: A Celebration of Creative Clothing.*

Other Fine Books From C&T Publishing

Appliqué 12 Easy Ways! Elly Sienkiewicz
The Art of Silk Ribbon Embroidery, Judith Montano
Christmas Traditions From the Heart, Volume Two, Margaret Peters
A Colorful Book, Yvonne Porcella
Colors Changing Hue, Yvonne Porcella
Dimensional Appliqué—Baskets, Blooms & Borders, Elly Sienkiewicz
Fantastic Figures: Ideas & Techniques Using the New Clays, Susanna Oroyan
14,287 Pieces of Fabrics and Other Poems, Jean Ray Laury
Heirloom Machine Quilting, Harriet Hargrave
Imagery on Fabric, Jean Ray Laury
Pattern Play, Doreen Speckmann
Pieced Clothing, Yvonne Porcella
Pieced Clothing Variations, Yvonne Porcella
Patchwork Quilts Made Easy, Jean Wells (co-published with Rodale)
Quilts for Fabric Lovers, Alex Anderson
Quilts, Quilts, and More Quilts! Diana McClun and Laura Nownes
Stitching Free: Easy Machine Pictures, Shirley Nilsson
Symmetry: A Design System for Quiltmakers, Ruth B. McDowell
Virginia Avery's Nifty Neckwear
Visions: Quilts, Layers of Excellence, Quilt San Diego
Wearable Art for Real People, Mary Mashuta

For more information write for a free catalog from
C&T Publishing
P.O. Box 1456
Lafayette, CA 94549
1-800-284-1114